MULTI-SENSORY SPELLING

101 Tips for Parents and Teachers

Peter O'Prey .   B.Ed. M.Ed PQHNI

Greater Expectations Learning Centre

Belfast.

N. Ireland

www.greaterexpectations.org.uk

Research shows there are an estimated 3 to 5 percent of school-age children with Attention Deficit Disorder/ADD/ADHD/Dyslexia. In response to the needs expressed by teachers for teaching strategies that work with these children, the U.S. Department of Education has supported research in classrooms to determine successful teaching techniques employed by elementary (primary) schoolteachers to keep children focused on task.

The following tips, for experienced and inexperienced elementary (primary) schoolteachers alike, are tried and true methods for reaching children with ADD/Dyslexia. Children with ADD/Dyslexia, typically have problems with inattention, impulsiveness, and hyperactivity. They often have difficulty paying attention in class and seem to shift aimlessly form one unfinished activity to another. These children generally appear restless, fidgeting constantly in their seats, playing with pencils or other objects, or disturbing nearby students. Many children with ADD/Dyslexia also have difficulty following their teacher's instructions or forming friendships with other children in the class. Like other children with disabilities, children with ADD/Dyslexia learn best when their teachers understand their special needs and individualise their educational program to meet these needs.

Peter O'Prey

The practices themselves should be a part of an educational program based around three key components - classroom accommodations, behaviour management and Individualised academic instruction. To make this as valuable a resource as possible, you should consider these three steps in developing an affective educational program for your student with ADD/Dyslexia.

- Evaluate the child's individual need

- Assess the unique educational needs of a child with ADD/Dyslexia with the teacher/.

- Working with a multi-disciplinary team, consider both academic and behavioural needs using formal diagnostic assessments and informal classroom observations. Parents need to get the school moving as quickly as possible.

- Select appropriate instructional practices. Determine which instructional practices will meet the academic behaviour needs you have identified for the child

- Select practices that fit the content are age appropriate and gain the co-operation of the child.

- Integrate appropriate practices within an individual program.

- Combine the practices you have selected into an Individual Educational Program, Plan how to integrate the educational activities provided to other children in your class with those selected for the child with ADD.

Because no two children with ADD/Dyslexia are alike, no single educational program or setting will be best for all the children. Academic Instruction Children with ADD/Dyslexia often have difficulty learning and achieving academically in school. Effective teachers consistently monitor the child and adapt and individualised academic instruction.

General Instructional Principles

Effective teachers help prepare their students to learn when they introduce, conduct and conclude each academic lesson. These principles of effective instruction, which reflect what we know about how to educate all children in the class, will especially help a child with ADD/Dyslexia to stay focused on his assigned tasks as he transitions for one lesson to another throughout the school day.

Students with ADD/Dyslexia benefit from clear statements about their teacher's expectations at the beginning of the lesson.

Consider these strategies:

- Review previous lessons.

- Review information about previous lesson on this topic. For example, remind children that yesterday's lesson focused on learning how to regroup in subtraction.

- Review several problems before describing the current lesson set learning expectations.

- State what students are expected to learn during the lesson. For example, explain to students that a language arts lesson will involve reading a story about Paul Bunyan and identifying new vocabulary words in the story.

- Set behavioural expectations. Describe how students are expected to behave during the lesson. For example, tell children that they may talk quietly to their neighbours as they work on a set-work assignment or raise their hands to get your attention.

- State needed materials. Identify all materials that the child will need during the lesson. For example, specify that children need their journals and pencils for journal writing or their crayons, scissors, and coloured paper for an art project; rather than leaving children to figure out on their own the materials required for a lesson.

- Explain additional resources. Tell students how to obtain help in mastering the lesson. For example, remind the children to refer to a particular page in the textbook to get help in completing a worksheet.

When conducting an academic lesson, effective teachers use some of the following strategies:

- Use Audio-Visual materials.
  Use a variety of audio-visual materials to present academic lessons. For example, use overhead

projector to demonstrate how to solve an addition problem requiring regrouping. The students can work on the problem at their desks, while you manipulate counters on the projector screen.

- Check Student Performance.
  Question individual students about their mastery of the lesson. For example, you can ask a student doing set-work to demonstrate how he or she arrived at the answer to a problem or ask individual students to state, in their own words, how the main character felt at the end of the story.

- Ask Probing Questions.
  Probe for the correct answer before calling on another student and allow children sufficient time to work out the answer in question. Count at least 15 seconds before giving the answer and ask follow-up questions that give the child an opportunity to demonstrate what he or she knows.

- Perform On-going Student Evaluation.
  Identify students who need additional assistance. Watch for signs of lack of comprehension, such as daydreaming or visual or verbal indications of frustration. Provide these children with extra explanation or ask another student to serve as a peer tutor for the lesson.

- Help Students Self-Correct Their Own Mistakes.
  Describe how students can identify and correct their own mistakes. For example, remind students that they should check their calculations in mathematic problems and reiterate how they can do that;

Peter O'Prey

remind students of particularly difficult spelling rules and how students can watch out for "easy-to-make" errors.

- Focus Dawdling Students.
  Remind students who dawdle to keep working and redirect these students to focus on their assigned task. For example, you can provide follow-up directions or assign learning partners. These practices can be directed at individual children or at the entire class.

- Lower Noise Level.
  Monitor the noise level in the classroom and provide corrective feedback, as needed. If the noise level exceeds the level appropriate for the type of lesson, remind all students - or individual students - about the behaviour rules stated at the beginning of the lesson.

Students with ADD/ADHD/Dyslexia often have difficulty refocusing their attention as they end one academic lesson and move on to the next lesson. Effective teachers help their students prepare for these transitions when concluding a lesson.

- Provide Advance Warnings.
  Provide advance warning that a lesson is about to end. Announce five or ten minutes prior to the end of the lesson (particularly for set-work and group projects) how much time remains. You may also want to tell students at the beginning of the lesson how much time they will have to complete it.

- Check Assignments.
  Check completed assignments for at least some students. Review with some students what they have learned during the lesson's, to get a sense of how ready the class was for the lesson and how to plan the next lesson.

- Preview the Next Lesson.
  Instruct students how to begin preparing for the next lesson. For example, inform children that they need to put away their textbooks and come to the front of the room for a large group spelling lesson.

Individualised Instructional Practices

Effective teachers individualise their instructional practices based on the needs of their students in different academic subjects. Students have different ways of getting information, not all of which involve traditional reading and listening. Individualised lessons in language arts, mathematics, and organisational skills benefit not only children with ADD/ADHD/Dyslexia, but also other children who have diverse learning needs.

Language Arts Reading Comprehension

To help children with ADD/ADHD/Dyslexia, who are poor readers, improve their reading comprehension skills, try the following instructional practices:

- Silent Reading Time.
  Establish a fixed time each day for silent reading (e.g., DEAR: Drop Everything And Read).

- Follow - Along Reading.
  Ask the child to read a story silently while listening to other students or the teacher read the story out loud to the entire class.

- Partner Reading Activities.
  Pair the child with ADD/ADHD with another student partner who is a stronger reader. The partners take turns reading orally and listening to each other.

- Storyboards.
  Ask the child to make storyboards that illustrate the sequence of main events in a story.

- Storytelling.
  Schedule "storytelling" sessions where the child can retell a story he or she has read recently.

- Play-Acting.
  Schedule "play-acting" sessions where the child can role-play different characters in a favourite story.

- Word bank.
  Keep a word bank or dictionary of new or "hard-to read" sight vocabulary words.

- Board Games for Reading Comprehension.
  Play board games that provide practice with target reading comprehension skills or sight vocabulary words.

- Computer Games for Reading Comprehension.
  Schedule computer time for the child to have "drill - and - practice" with sight vocabulary words.

Phonics and Grammar

To help children with ADD/ADHD/Dyslexia, master phonics and grammar rules, the following are effective:

- Mnemonics for Phonics and Grammar.
  Teach the child mnemonics that provide reminders about hard-to-learn grammatical rules such as (a) correct punctuation, (b) irregular verb tenses, and (c) correct capitalisation.

- Word Families.
  Teach the child to recognize and read word families that illustrate particular phonetic concepts (e.g., 'ph" sounds).

- "Everyday" Examples of Grammar Rules.
  Take advantage of naturally occurring events to teach grammar rule skills in the context of everyday life. For example, ask a boy and a girl who are reading a story together questions about the proper use of male and female pronouns.

- Board Games for Phonics and Grammar.
  Play board games that practice phonetically irregular words.

- Computer Games for Phonics and Grammar.
  Use a computer to provide opportunities to have "drill - and practice" with phonics or grammar lessons.

- Structured Programs for Phonics and Grammar.
  Teach phonics and grammar skills through a structured program such as Dyslexia Action (UK) "Units of Sound" program.

Peter O'Prey

Writing

In composing stories or other writing assignments, children with ADD/ADHD/Dyslexia benefit from the following practices:

- Standards for Writing Assignments.
  Identify and teach the child classroom - wide standards for acceptable written work.

- Recognising Parts of a Story.
  Teach the student how to describe the major parts of a story (e.g., plot, main characters, setting, conflict, and resolution).

- Post Office.
  Establish a "post office" in the classroom and provide students with opportunities to write, mail, and receive letters to and from their classmates and teacher.

- Visualising Compositions.
  Ask the child to close his or her eyes and visualise a paragraph that the teacher reads aloud. Another variation of this technique is to ask a student to describe a recent event while the other students have their eyes closed.

To help children with ADD/ADHD/Dyslexia, who are poor spellers master their spelling lessons, the following have been found to be useful.

- Teaching Frequently Used Spelling Words.
  Assign spelling words that the child routinely uses in his or hers speech each day.

- Creating a Dictionary of Misspelled Words.
  Ask the child to keep a personal dictionary of frequently misspelled words.

- Using Partner Spelling Activities.
  Pair the child with another student. Ask the partners to quiz each other about how to spell new words. Encourage both students to guess the correct spelling.

- Working with Manipulatives.
  Use cut out letters or other manipulatives to spell out hard-to-learn words.

- Using Colour-Coded Letters.
  Colour code different letters in "hard-to-spell" words (e.g. receipt).

- Using "Movement Activities".
  Combine movement activities with spelling lessons (e.g. jump rope while spelling the word out loud).

- Using "Everyday" Examples of Hard-To-Spell Words.
  Take advantage of naturally occurring events to teach difficult spelling words in context. For example, ask a child eating a cheese sandwich to spell "sandwich".

Handwriting

Students with ADD/ADHD/Dyslexia, who have difficulty with manuscript or cursive writing benefit from these instructional practices:

- Individual Chalkboards.
  Ask each child to practice copying and erasing the

target words on a small, individual chalkboard. Two children can be paired to practice their target words together.

- Quiet Places for Handwriting.
  Provide the child with a special "quiet place" (e.g. on a table outside the classroom) to complete his or her handwriting assignments.

- Spacing Words on a Page.
  Teach the child to use his or her finger to measure how much space to leave between each word in a written assignment.

- Special Writing Paper.
  Ask the child to use special paper with vertical lines to learn to space letters and words on a page.

- Tape Recorders.
  Ask the student to dictate writing assignments into a tape recorder.

- Dictating Writing Assignments.
  Have the teacher or another student write down a story told by a child with ADD/ADHD/Dyslexia.

- Structured Programs for Handwriting.
  Teach handwriting skills through a structured program, such as Jan Olson's "Handwriting Without Tears" program.

Mathematics

There are several individualised instructional practices that can help children with ADD/ADHD/Dyslexia, improve their basic computation skills. The following are just a few:

- Recognising Patterns in Mathematics.
  Teach the student to recognise patterns when adding, subtracting, multiplying, or dividing whole numbers.

- Partner Mathematics Activities.
  Pair a child with AD/ADHD/Dyslexia, with another student and provide opportunities for the partners to quiz each other about basic computation skills.

- Mnemonics for Basic Computation.
  Teach the child mnemonics that describe basic steps in computing whole numbers. For example. "Don't Miss Susie's Boot" can be used to help the student recall the basic steps in long division (i.e. divide, multiply, subtract and bring down).

- "Real Life" Examples of Money Skills.
  Provide the child with naturally occurring "real life" opportunities to practice target money skills. For example, ask the child to calculate his or her change when paying for lunch in the school cafeteria.

- Colour Coding Arithmetic Symbols.
  Colour code basic arithmetic symbols such as +, -, and = to provide visual cues for children when they are computing whole numbers.

- Using Calculators to Check Basic Computation.
  Ask the child to use a calculator to check his addition, subtraction, multiplication, or division

- Board Games for Basic Computation.
  Ask the child to play board games to practice adding, subtracting, multiplying and dividing whole numbers.

- Computer Games for Basic Computation.
  Schedule computer time for the child for "drill-and-practice" with basic computation facts.

- Structured Programs for Basic Computation.
  Teach basic computation skills through a structured program such as Innovative Learning Concepts' "Touch Moth" program.

Solving Word Problems

To help children with ADD/ADHD/Dyslexia, improve their skill in solving word problems in mathematics, try the following:

- Rereading the Problem.
  Teach the child to read a word problem two times before beginning to compute the answer.

- Using Clue Words.
  Teach the child "clue words" that identify which operation to use when solving word problems. For example, words such as "sum," "total," or "all together" may indicate an addition operation.

- Mnemonics for Word Problems.
  Teach students mnemonics that help remind them of basic questions to ask in solving word problems (e.g. what is the question asked in the problem, what information do you have to figure out the

answer, and what operation should you use to compute the answer).

- "Real Life" Examples of Word Problems.
  Ask the student to create and solve word problems that provide practice with specific target operations such as addition, subtraction, multiplication or division. These problems can be based on recent "real life" events in the children's lives.

- Using Calculators to Check Word Problems.
  Ask the student to use a calculator to check his or her answers to assigned word problems.

Special Materials

Some children with ADD/ADHD/Dyslexia benefit from using special materials to help them complete their mathematics assignments.

- Number Lines.
  Provide a number line for the child to use when computing whole numbers.

- Manipulatives.
  Use manipulatives to help students gain basic computation skills such as counting poker chips when adding single-digit numbers.

- Graph Paper.
  Ask the child to use graph paper to help organise columns when adding, subtracting, multiplying or dividing whole numbers.

Organisational Skills

Many students with ADD/ADHD/Dyslexia are easily distracted and have difficulty focusing their attention on assigned tasks. However, there are several practices that can help children with ADD/ADHD/Dyslexia improve their organisation of homework and other daily assignments.

- Assignment Notebook.
  Provide the child with an assignment notebook to help organise homework and other set-work.

- Colour-Coded Folders.
  Provide the child with colour-coded folders to help organise assignments for different academic subjects (e.g. reading, mathematics, social science and science).

- Homework Partners.
  Assign the child a partner to help record homework and other set-work in the proper folders and assignment notebook.

- Cleaning Out Desks and Book Bags.
  Ask the child to periodically sort through and clean out his or her desk, book bag, and other special places where written assignments are stored.

Children with ADD/ADHD/Dyslexia, who have difficulty finishing their assignments on time can also benefit from individualised instruction that helps them improve their time management skills.

- Using a Wristwatch.
  Teach the child how to read and use a wristwatch to

manage his or her time when completing assigned work.

- Using a Calendar.
  Teach the child how to read and use a calendar to schedule his or her assignments.

- Practicing Sequencing Activities.
  Provide the child with supervised opportunities to break down a long assignment into a sequence of short, interrelated activities.

- Creating a Daily Activity Schedule.
  Tape schedule of planned daily activities to the child's desk.

- Study Skills Using Venn Diagrams.
  Teach a child with ADD/ADHD/Dyslexia, how to use Venn diagrams to help illustrate and organise key concepts in reading, mathematics or other academic subjects.

- Note-Taking Skills.
  Teach a child with ADD/ADHD/Dyslexia, how to take notes when organising key academic concepts that he or she has learned with a program such as Anita Archer's "Skills for Schools Success".

- Developing a Checklist of Frequent Mistakes.
  Provide the child with a checklist of mistakes that he or she frequently makes in written assignments (e.g. punctuation or capitalisation errors), mathematics (e.g. addition or subtraction errors), or other academic subjects. Teach the child how to use this

list when proof-reading his or her work at home or school.

- Using a Checklist of Homework Supplies.
  Provide the child with a checklist that identifies categories of items needed for homework assignments (e.g. books, pencils, and homework assignment sheets).

- Preparing Uncluttered Workspace.
  Teach a child with ADD/ADHD/ Dyslexia how to prepare an uncluttered workspace to complete his assignments. For example, instruct the child to clear away unnecessary books or other materials before beginning a set-work assignment.

- Monitoring Homework Assignments.
  Keep track of how well your students with ADD/ADHD/Dyslexia complete their assigned homework. Discuss and resolve with them and their parents any problems in completing these assignments. For example, evaluate the difficulty of the assignments and how long the children spend on their homework each night.

Behaviour Management

Children with ADD/ADHD/Dyslexia often are impulsive and hyperactive. Effective teachers use behaviour management techniques to help these children learn how to control their behaviour:

- Verbal Reinforcement.
  Students with ADD/ADHD/Dyslexia benefit from frequent reinforcement of appropriate behaviour

and correction of inappropriate behaviour. Verbal reinforcement takes on the form of praise and reprimands. In addition, it is sometimes helpful to selectively ignore inappropriate behaviour.

- Verbal Praise.
  Simple phrases such as "good job" encourage a child to act appropriately. Praise children frequently, and look for a behaviour to praise before - not after - a child is off task.

- Verbal Reprimands.
  Do not hesitate to request that a child change his or her behaviour. The most effective reprimands are brief and directed at te child's behaviour - not at the child.

- Selective Ignoring of Inappropriate Behaviour.
  Carefully evaluate whether to intervene when a child misbehaves. In some instances, it is helpful to ignore the child's inappropriate behaviour, particularly if a child is misbehaving to get your attention.

Effective teachers also use behavioural prompts with their students with ADD/ADHD/Dyslexia, as well as with other students in the class. These prompts help remind students about your expectations for their leaning and behaviour in the classroom:

- Visual Cues.
  Establish simple, non-intrusive visual cues to remind the child to remain on task. For example, you can point at the child while looking him or her in the

eye, or hold out your hand, palm down, near the child.

- Proximity Control.
  When talking to a child, move to where the child is standing or sitting. Your physical proximity to the child will help the child to focus and pay attention to what you are saying.

Counselling

In some instances, children with ADD/ADHD/Dyslexia need counselling to learn how to manage their own behaviour:

- Classroom Interviews.
  Discuss how to resolve social conflicts with classroom interviews. Conduct impromptu counselling sessions with one student or a small group of students in the classroom where the conflict arises. In this setting, ask two children who are arguing about a game to discuss how to settle their differences. Encourage the children to resolve their problems by talking to each other, while you quietly monitor their interaction during the interview.

- Social Skills Classes.
  Teach children with ADD/ADHD/Dyslexic appropriate social skills using a structured pullout class. For example, you can ask the children to role-play and model different solutions to common social problems. It is critical to provide for the generalisation of these skills, including structured

opportunities for the children to use the social skills they learn.

For some children with ADD/ADHD/Dyslexia, behavioural contracts, tangible rewards, or token economy systems are helpful in teaching them how to manage their own behaviour. Because students' individual needs are different, it is important for teachers to evaluate whether these practices are appropriate for their classrooms.

- Behavioural Contract.
  Identify specific academic or behavioural goals for the child with ADD/ADHD/Dyslexia. Work together with the child to co-operatively identify appropriate goals such as completing homework assignments on time and obeying safety rules on the school playground. Take the time to ensure that the child agrees that his or her goals are important to master.

- Tangible Rewards.
  Use tangible rewards to re-enforce appropriate behaviour. These rewards can include (a) stickers such as "happy faces" or sports teams emblems or (b) privileges, such as extra time on the computer or lunch with the teacher. In some cases, you may be able to enlist the support of parents in rewarding the children at home.

- Token Economy System.
  Use token economy systems to motivate a child to achieve a goal identified in a behavioural contract. For example, a child can earn points for each homework assignment completed on time. In some

cases, students also lose points for each homework assignment not completed on time. After earning a specified number of points, the student receives a tangible reward such as extra time on a computer or a 'free period" on Friday afternoon.

Classroom Accommodations

Many children with ADD/ADHD/Dyslexia benefit from accommodations that reduce distractions in the classroom environment. These accommodations, which include modifications within both the physical environment and learning environment of the classroom, help some children with ADD/ADHD/Dyslexia stay on task and learn. Accommodations of the physical environment include determining where a child with ADD/ADHD/Dyslexia will sit in the classroom. There are two main types of special seat assignments:

- Seat Near the Teacher.
  Assign a child a seat near your desk or in front of the room. This seat assignment provides opportunities for you to monitor and reinforce the child's on task behaviour.

- Seat Near a Student Role Model.
  Assign a child a seat near a student role model. This seat arrangement provides opportunities for children to work cooperatively and learn from their peers in the class.

Effective teachers also use different environmental prompts to make accommodations with in the physical environment of the classroom:

- Hand Gestures.
  Use hand signals to communicate privately with a child with ADD/ADHD/Dyslexia. For example, ask the child to raise his or her hand every time you ask a question. A closed fist can signal that the child knows the answer; an open palm can signal that he or she does not know the answer. You would call on the child to answer only when he or she makes a fist.

- Egg Timers.
  Note for the children the time at which the lesson is starting and the time at which it will conclude. Set a timer to indicate to children how much time remains in the lesson and place it at the front of the classroom; the children can check the timer to see how much time remains. Interim prompts can be used as well. For instance, children can monitor their own progress during a 30-minute lesson if the timer is set for 10 minutes 3 times.

- Classroom Lights.
  Turning the classroom lights "on and off" prompts children that the noise level in the room is too high and they should be quiet. This practice can also be used to signal that it is time to begin preparing for the next lesson.

- Music.
  Play music on a tape recorder or chords on a piano

to prompt children that they are too noisy. In addition, playing different types of music on a tape recorder communicates to children what level of activity is appropriate for a particular lesson. For example, play quiet classical music for quiet set-activities and jazz for active group activities.

Effective teachers make accommodations in the learning environment by guiding children with ADD/ADHD/Dyslexia with follow-up directions:

- Follow-up Oral Directions.
  After giving directions to the class as a whole, provide additional, oral directions for a child with ADD/ADHD/Dyslexia. For example, ask the child if he or she understood the directions, and repeat the direction together.

- Follow-up Written Direction.
  Provide follow-up directions in writing. For example, write the page number for an assignment on the blackboard. You can remind the child to look at the blackboard if he or she forgets the assignment.

Effective teachers also use special instructional tools to modify the classroom-learning environment and accommodate the special needs of their students with ADD/ADHD/Dyslexia.

- Highlighting Key Words.
  Highlight key words in the instructions on worksheets to help the child with ADD/ADHD/Dyslexia focus on the directions. You can prepare the worksheet before the lesson begins

or underline key words as you and the child read the directions together.

- Using Pointers.
  Teach the child to use a pointer to help visually track written words on a page. For example, provide the child with a bookmark to help him or her follow along when students are taking turns reading aloud.

- Adapting Worksheets.
  Teach a child how to adapt instructional worksheets. For example, help a child fold his or her reading worksheet to reveal only one question at a time. The child can also use a blank piece of paper to cover the other questions on the page.

Does your child have a learning difficulty? Signs to look for ...

- Warning is to watch for are poor handwriting, poor reading comprehension and poor organisational skills.

- If your child doesn't enjoy reading, says schoolwork is boring, is labelled or is always the class clown, they may be trying to covet-up their inability to read and write.

- If your child suffers from low self-esteem or behavioural problems, such as tantrums, or is withdrawn, they may be frustrated by their inability to read and write but too embarrassed to say so.

- Be aware these signs also indicate problems other then learning difficulties. Children can fail behind in class if they can't see to the front of the room or can't hear their teachers. Have your children checked for long-sightedness, ear infections and allergies.

- Sit down with your kids as they do their homework to get an idea of their progress.

- If you think your, child may have a learning difficulty please do not hesitate to contact this Trust, family Doctor, or Specialist ..... talk to the schoolteacher's to enable yourself to advocate for your child.
  Personal statement
  I would look first at an Educational Assessment, with on Educational Psychologist, who is able to determine the learning age level, the child is able to comprehend.

Practising Spellings At Home

It is really important that parents and caregivers are involved in helping children to learn their spellings.
Confidence in spelling allows children to write more freely and imaginatively.
You should practise your spellings for 10 to 20 minutes EVERY day.
Here are some games or ideas you could use.
Why not try a different one each night to keep it fun and interesting.
Remember everyone learns by;

<u>Doing it, seeing it, saying it, writing/drawing it, listening to it</u>
so making sure you have variety of games and tasks is a great way to ensure the learning sticks!

The Best 30 Methods

Using a multisensory approach can often develop by trial and error. You suddenly find a method that suits your child. The important thing to remember is making it fun. These thirty approaches help foster retention of spellings which is often a problem

1) Word Search
Create your own word searches using your spelling words. Or use this link to get your computer to do it for you. http://puzzlemaker.discoveryeducation.com/WordSearch SetupForm.asp

2) Draw your words on Lite-Brite.
http://www.sfpg.com/animation/liteBrite.html#%7CHERE

3) Air spelling:
Choose a spelling word. With your index finger write the word in the air slowly, say each letter. Your parent needs to remind you that you need to be able to 'see' the letters you have written in the air. When you have finished writing the word underline it and say the word again. Now get you parents to ask you questions the about the word. For example they could ask 'What is the first letter?' 'What is the last letter?' 'How many letters are there?' etc.

4) Media Search:
Using a newspaper or magazine you have 15 minutes to look for your spelling words. Circle them in different coloured crayon. Which of your spellings words was used the most times?

5) Shaving Cream Practice:
An easy way to clean those dirty tables is to finger paint on them with shaving cream. Squirt some on the table (with your parents' permission and supervision!) and then practice spelling your words by writing them with your finger in the shaving cream.

6) Salt Box Spelling:
Ask your parents pour salt into a shallow box or tray (about 3cm deep) and then practice writing you spellings in it with your finger.

7) Scrabble Spelling:
Find the letters you need to spell you words and then mix them up in the bag. Get your parents to time you unscrambling your letters. For extra maths practice you could find out the value of each of you words.

8) Pyramid Power:
Sort your words into a list from easiest to hardest. Write the easiest word at the top of the page near the middle. Write the next easiest word twice underneath. Write the third word three times underneath again until you have built your pyramid

9) Ransom Note:
Cut the letters needed to for your words from a newspaper or magazine and glue them down to spell the words.

10) Spell It With Beans:
Use Lima beans (or any dried beans or lentils) to spell out your words. If you glue them onto separate pieces of card then you made a great set of flash cards to practice with for the rest of the week.

11) Pipe Cleaners Or Tooth Picks:
These are just a couple of suggestions of things you could use to for your spelling words.

12) Tasty Words:
Just like above but this time try and find tasty things to spell your words with, like raisins. Then when you spell them right you get to eat them!

13) Design A Word:
Pick one word and write it in bubble letters. Colour in each letter in a different pattern.

14) Sign Your Word:
Practice spelling your words by signing each letter.
Many schools these days teach basic sign language. It may be useful to learn some of the techniques. Most cities run courses . In the UK try
http://www.british-sign.co.uk/

15) Water wash:
Use a paintbrush and water to write your words outside on concrete or pavements.

16) ABC Order:
Write your words out in alphabetical order. Then write them in reverse alphabetical order.

17) Story Time:
Write a short using all your words. Don't forget to check your punctuation!

18) Simple Sentence:
Write a sentence for each of your words. Remember each sentence must start with a capital letter and end with a full stop.

19) Colourful Words:
Use two different coloured pens to write your words. One to write the consonants and one to write the vowels. Do this a couple of times then write the whole word in one colour.

20) Memory Game:
Make pairs of word cards. Turn them all over and mix them up. flip over two cards, if they match you get to keep them, if not you have to turn them over again. Try and match all the pairs.

21) Finger Tracing:

Use your finger to spell out each of your words on your mum or dad's back. Then it's their turn to write the words on your back for you to feel and spell.

22) Spelling Steps:
Write your words as if they were steps, adding one letter each time. (It's much easier doing this on squared paper)

23) Scrambled Words:
Write your words then write them again with all the letters mixed up.

24) X-Words:
Find two of your spelling words with the same letter in and write them so they criss cross.

25) Ambidextrous:
Swap your pen into the hand that you don't normally write with. Now try writing out your spellings with that hand.

26) Telephone Words:
Translate your words into numbers from the telephone keypad.

27) Secret Agent:
Write out the alphabet, and then give each letter a different number from 1 to 26. (a = 1, b = 2, c = 3 ect.) Now you can spell out your words in secret code.

28) Missing Letters:

Ask your mum or dad to write out one of your words loads of times on piece of paper, but each time they have to miss out a letter or two. Then you have to fill in the missing letters. After you have checked them all try it again with another word.

29) Listen Carefully:
Ask your parents to spell out one of your words then you have to say what the word is they've spelt out.

30) Acrostic:
Use words that start with each letter in you spelling word. You're more likely to remember it if it makes sense!

Printed in Great Britain
by Amazon